T0161392

night  ox
Jordan Scott

Coach House Books, Toronto

first edition

 Canada Council   Conseil des Arts
for the Arts   du Canada

Published with the generous assistance of the Canada Council
for the Arts and the Ontario Arts Council. Coach House
Books also acknowledges the support of the Government of
Canada through the Canada Book Fund and the Government
of Ontario through the Ontario Book Publishing Tax Credit.

LIBRARY AND ARCHIVES CANADA CATALOGUING IN
PUBLICATION

Scott, Jordan, 1978-, author
      Night & ox / Jordan Scott.

ISBN 978-1-55245-329-2 (paperback).

      I. Title. II. Title: Night and ox.

PS8587.C6254N55 2016   C811'.6   C2016-904398-3

Night & Ox is available as an ebook: ISBN 978 1 77056 483 1

'Comrade, I beg you to tie me
To that tree there and bind my thighs tight.'

– Bertolt Brecht, 'Ballad of Friendship'

For Summer, Sacha and Rowan

sunny edge
of outcry's
tastic harpsichord
my pleasure
eellike
living
in hostile
sorrow
in unfulfilled
mornings
come osteoderm
necklace clutching, come
pissant sphere
of root position
live sweetly
unownered deer
bubbles, stick
finger lake
taser azure
nightdress
you're in

heartbreak

breathable

flourish

slake

calm

mouth

eyebite

loganberries vein

comet wrote

carnate

wiretap lip

fistula tizzy

circus cell

blazeday

break by

dying

between day

dark

and proton

bouquet plankton

earworm

sunspot

fulm and flume

windchill reflex

starlit parsnips

frill underfur

cushion croaks

elm

luminous

seasand

claspers

scapegrace
deep
blowhole
bandwidth sheesh
liken
this
feeling
aquatile sun
trialect
snotpaper's
night-shirting
cuttlefish
the
coil
I
am
mouth
I
am
silt still
planetoid
fruitfulness
instagramming
stratosphere's
whirl
brick dust
milk powder
milk me
facesplitting
beehive
purpler

than
cupcakes
purple
subroutines
I
sleep
street
drain
seems italic
strikethrough
night
lunacy
or
rivery
rubs
alone
ankle nude
long
lines
of
lynx
scat
we're
in
we're
snowsleep
flurry mask
my
chant
to
follow

your
placenta
a
meadow
my
self
a
boy
licking
plate's
massacre
patterns
twenty
thin
strokes
October
trackless
October
throw
boybird
blissed
any subtext
sacral
reaching any
table, grape
sacral
covered
mustard
stone
should
I

ever
feel
wonder
again
colossal
leg cluster
string drown
infant
lake
system
nervous
voltage
swap
vogue
my
bedwhole
loch
my
spur-fat
juiced vapour
spur Sockeye
egging
hormone snag
spur glottal
gland oil
juiced vapour
green sweat
waterboard
heartache
it's eggskull
tiny blot

vortices
agalaxia tiptoes
because
I
say
so
you're
onthrob's anthill
and flickout
perfect a scale
I cede dysfluent
one seme
as dessert spoonfuls away
tinder drone
rain
cinder pomace
sodden
thermometer lyric
you tinarsed silly
conjure loitering
sackdawn weep
fuselage
displode
urchin, means
days done
transhuman
truncheon
Pac-Man
hatchetal
encyclicals
and all

the kissmore
and all
don't
let me
out
of myself
but
krill me
completely
dully
full duty
neutrinos
jackknife
soulcake
I'm
exhumanistically
sorry
for
almost
nothing
shapes
like
lip
piss
I
ravish
tuck
in hide
nor tail
your
life

battling

breezehands

full

gibbon raid

shit

me

word

batholes

skip-rope

memory

rooms

of

I

will

go

to

my

desk

silently

sit

hewn

to

tongueflop

until

it's

what

sign

a

stanzaic

glade

or

sign
a
morning
labyrinth
skeletal
infinity
I
tear
you
apart
for
pleasure
for
love
lies
gangrene
deadgone
waves
out the when
of the window
I'm
leaving
for
work
repeat
calendar
out
lasting
mom's
driftface
can't

I
say
under
what
lack
of
what
nature
quiet
of
petroglyphic tilts
terraforming lung's
ocean cyst
diveout
jelly seconds
go suck
mulligatawny
go suck
an egg
fib snout
browbeating
moonscape's
retinal clementines
acoustic
terracotta
lunascious
moonsmooth
goudasphere
tarsal fin
pixie sand
morning

elemental

buttbite

I'm

daylight's moonballoon

invaginal

kelprut

woodwork

slime sundress

murrain and

nonpsychic

shuteye

chickendeeds

are waterless

rawness

fore-scent

fluorescent

blissfulhead

wick

of pillowlips

albuminous

scorched

wormhole slur

slight Pleroma

it's form

for longing

for

slaughter

yes

everything's

vestibular sac

looms ungula

beeclouds
untwist
cosmonauts
unclench
hailstones
you
fresh
cataclysm prolix whispering
asteriod
lunchbox
stucco
twinkle
sandpaper body
inside mystical
alones
I
worry
about this
rosepink
compression
of love-dread
reads me
infrasound
coyote tolling
upstairs
jammies
nightie
burrowing
pupshins
backlit
ankylosaurus

you're small
your small
so cry's
inky stampede
blotchy
in bee
costume
in
glyph kitchen
on
glottis island
studded
sturgeon
weighs
dashberry
mirror drum
decimal
cosmoglottal
mudstone, look
borealis
it's crystalline
starboard boyform
metadata tone
boxlip
salmonoid
heaviness
always
magnetic
dignity
unlicked
cub

moments curious

unsinned

celestial

bodies'

spacecraft shot

missed trachea scoop

indulgence for

nightlight's

haywire tongues

synth languor

synthetic labour

silhouetting

silkbait

you

fluoroscope

forest bit

off supraglacial

half

articulate

melt

me linguistically

you're Hephæstus

your Hephæstus

minibar mind

jam ejecta

on kitchen floor

we

wet

the

bed

bedwet cuffs

truckpattern
makebelieve face
wants throughseek
hypotenuse
nixed tundra
nowmind
so geodynamic
gangplank
ablaze
I
hear
now
through
shower
vomit
sunsplash
cooed
sensual
hurried
titlight
my
wallet
my
weave
my
dadabear
biting my
chewing
aircrystal's
pronunciation
nasty

moveless
gloam
demands
lutefish
notch
gravity
encode
a sunbath
a firebath
a hanging
yet lip
intoxicatingly
kneedeep
balsamic
beyond
semitones
encode
a squid's
renaissance
leaves shiver
shrink
back to predawn
my
day too
blurred to
unread too
quiet
river be
quiet body
ache parasail
glittering

water fracture
semi blowhole
for day
shreds
physics
intestine
sea
a Dungeness
fantasticating
onward
electromagnetism's
torsos wheatmeal
when drown
can't resist
lettering
craves
and

finally, I think
the horde
is edible flowers

too young
to tomb
in echo
too young
to surrender shrimpish body
move to overhead
sonosphere rainbow
numbskull
gravity null

clusters seagrass
coloured
percolate
thrombolytic
body pore
nothing
subesophageal
but waste
and anguish
and ravenous
redclay
and assload
sincerity
my mean face
seeing you seeing
clouds underlit pink
windmill bilocating cornflakes
beachcombing hymn
cryptology pools
foamchild
screensaver
daybreak, quiet
it's cinderblock
notions
lingerie mosslike
tent
in substratum's
elusive butterfly
mouth
I'm
shadowhunting

under glacier
I'm
Lego jitters
Jell-O
boundary
off daybreak
scowl's
symmetry
I
can't
see
coming
to
bed
as
art
big
toe
in
syllable
scenery
in
no
milk
and
out
wasting
my
life
in
root

position
in
primate
streak
in
gloom
cut
meteor
chord
cruel
chime
chimerically
magnificent
supernanny
of cruel
gravity
spaceborne
embodiments netted
in chandelier yarn
swallow embodies
rose's mitochondrial
nightwork
sonnet logarithms
leaning up against
Broc or Donato
or watching
sea cucumbers or bushtits
die in form like magnetized
candy for tomorrow
eating daylike
letters in

cold bedmilk
ran down
leg little
ones underling
things too
will become
me in feeling
blue and iron chaoses
mock cheeses
of linen
beer aside
a body
a bog's
penitence
lilac blowtorches
goldrush esophagus
veins luxury
fluvial prose
processions to reservoirs
transonic thirsting
this skin digital
gleam
I
coagulate
deadlights
upload a forest grove, the lukewarm assess
the loving cereals
it's lassitude I'm under
fierce bric-a-brac
of moment's
see my walleyed love

of nature
my skullful
carps and tears
perfecting snowdrop
isn't beastling
down there
isn't cumblotch
enharmonic fern
valence
sea kitchen
bodies sledding
Titanomachy seeing
exhuminating small
riverbanks'
placate
strato-volcanoes
cello blast
exeunt
linguistically owed
epigram
so berry so
wildlife carols
waterproofing
mezzanine's sweet bristle
tonsils listless hills
and from so much thinking
I have
given my mouth
it's slowing
me down
beetledogs

play music
overloaded
biogluttony
blows away
corn smut
smouldering timber
landscape infectious
idleness
limb homebody
plying fungus
little necksnack
flung curve
kid fodder
leaves love's
uneven sound
and sound
moves survival
oxygen's fall
burns
shitforbrains
bottle din
membrane
crackers
interstellar
breakages
all them
I'm
given
I'm
lisping
I'm

you freerange you
musclepuff
zygomorphic
fleshquiff
so tremoring
little body
case hiss
swallowtailed
mouths vole
bent-over purge

the hawkeyes, the frescoing, the maze, your midrash
the prayers, the tenderloin, the trash, your hairbrain
the narrating, the naturalisms, the animalcules retrenching
the both us, our slippering, the velodromes in breath

bonkers canyon
booming dreamtime
sorta crayfish
unsleeping irradiance
perhaps I say
sorta hypnotically
bodies hand over
giving so much
omnivore so
fatherhooded
wilderness vine
gropes glowworm
ghosted womb-ways
wordsting sonogram
brightshines away

your first

moments

trespass

jubilant

breathing

people

shadows

aphid milk

papoose coccoon

rockheaping

airpower's quailpipe

painfulness

growing up

rampage

roused

gelatin

unthinkingly

tetherended

autumn

in aluminum diapers

sudden piano

needed to

touch it

to know

your own

mindshies

blemisheyes

timescale

radicalized

impediment poplars

the birch I break

for river
when next
to you
nothing in
nothing is
watercell
sleeps nor
captive
latitudinal
angiosperms
untangle
bedplay
bulls play ox
xo play
sinewcising
waterstrap
tickletorture
as if no more
touch
pleases
unsound
pleasures
blowtorch
river stencils
pitchforked
eucalypt's skin
sweven, a dream
a vision awake
drowned child
who swallows
dictum

divinities who
ride a bike
who dictum
this undoes
all day
you've been
at
it
all
along
good
for
nothing
fable
over
mountain
over
me
on
floor
mouth
the
tourbillon
world
flourish
of
farewell
to
sound
sound
and

sound
alone
finds
our
pisspoor
yard
my
lost
nœsis
the one
thing
in
time
I
want
is
fixed
in
feeling's
opera glass
tribunal
prism
body
close
too
hounded
hare
and
my
cell
lit

memory
of
no
shadowy
crustaceans
no
too skinny
three-year-old
boy
for
whom
I
sit
quietly
and
will
heart
un
ending
if
I'd
starve
precipitous
birds
over
a
nook
ravine
I
cannot
hold

no
trace
no
instant
no
of
no
who
was
dad
but
man's
dress
a
diary
catapult
above
a
non-mansion
magnitude
of glaciers
beatbox pare
laminæ rine
global ligature
make this
wheat you've
dropped
grubstakes
antfights
upon us
unsweetened lake

wound of this
fox's red-eye
eyeing nestbites
coal's cryptogram
dumbed spirit
I
barely inhabit
my
body
houses
containing
visions
of
houses
of
a
sit still
Summer
I
think
of
anything
I
can
to
slow
humid
mornings
in
blaring
touch

you
soulsuck
my
child
my gooseneck
remember
our
gardens
then
the
dark
ace
came
down
boughs
reach
hinder
look
watch
closer
someone
is
in
our
bed
across
light
to
crawl
to
thwart

everything

sea-purse

into

actual

treescape

is

ruinational

complexions of snails

convexing some aperture

mucous cape

morphology snaily

turtledove gall

beachfrost

plummet

when told

intimacy

gone form

lagoons clutching

hillful rammed

strand loop

earth's

inescapable

speechreach

I

want

this

sound

of

capture

bellybitten

moan

stutterkiss
in
blithe
scorpion
some
endless
typhoon
spill
I
here
endless
obedience
forms
sight
wounding
longer
I
wait
for
little
things
to
cross
a
threshold
unsounds
with all its underfoot
hoof gone running
with all its cherry juice
and foxfur hush
wishbone hill

clutching

lagoons

carload

glottalkids

cuffed lark

speechmaking

mommy brigades

gathering air

burning leaf

edible instant

at such

mercy

forms

cocapillary

scree cerulean

window

halves sound

mesocyclone

coldroll

oatclap tryst

explosion

minefields

aplomb

this morning

barfed tresses

prosthesis sun

flykilling

allocution

as tragedienne

redbricked

but inactitude

still-mouth
popping velvet
sound
and sound and
soundsound
moves
moonskin
wolf of the story
tinges of me
recorded ravine
drawn geometrical
against nightlight
mitochondrial
ferticule, poeticule
fern coos the
climax forest
for silence is
I
am
nothing
not
a
notch
colour
of
floral
but
not
the
chroma
but

waits
for
all
entrance
gnashing
crib
patterns
chant
sequitur
dim
wire
sequitur
burying
creek's
watercheek
in
hand
I
often
think
I
am
too
far
too
lean
souled
too
dull
shells
of

half
my
face

the scrotums, and dungeons, the browsing modalities
the snacktime, and workshirts, the loving requestioning

some minuscule
orb some toe
footdigit
under leaf
under us
satellite cuss
that night
in my hand
phytoplankton
moonsong
flashbulb
zoolicks
undercloth
downpour
entrails
shelling, etcetera
clam prattle
muscle some
fetishistic puddle
birds for birder
look
it's
ruined
animal purity

silly
behind cosmos
slashed trail
dogfollow
blurting
abeyance
I
type stupor
broken woodland
I'm lost in
flowerchart
birthstone
woundsore laminæ
planned pebbles
gaze feet
before entering
coniferous
jerkoff
pumpkin
be dazzled
salmon
gauzesea
riverlips no more
than sleep is
afloat
I
to the mobile secretions
I perforating thrush
pussywhips
I their flavours
henbane

divinity
I antiorbital slick
antiviral noose
I am a boy
on a beach
on a pincushion
kelpbed dadbod
mellow grapevines
through pillow
waterbed
grass cut grow
want lawn treble
want shear
landscape duty
clinical vocal
deft wombs
phonocule
bionic cosmogonies I
to electroluminescence
say groping is wrath err
our polarity
locks our
stutter frostwork
rectify galaxy's nonviolent stammer
I'm
boogeyman's
house, sty
nightgown
ravine everything
legumes matchbox
boy in lightyear's

entrail's equinox
purring kid sounds
translunar and
clay parsec
I'm
my son's deerhound
skin in barleycorn
surplussage
of
prey
soffit
flames
fluoroscopy
silvers
incoherent
greenloads
hunting face
shady blue
space current
when that seal
washed up
New Brighton
translucence
siege engined
tethered pores
away with words
remember how we
mono-pile Pacific
digging vein
such silence
and nothing

wakes
blubber
writhe
world
you're in
my jacket
my waistband
my downvest
short-haired
you are
supraglacial
a gladis
veins
refolded obelisk
an hour
you walk
insignificant chromata
flood small clothes
flykilling venous
dizziness
weathervane
cavities tenderloin
tetrachord
simple as genes
well, wood, lace
sticks bowel
hounds mythical
tantrums' crass gorgeousness
cross lustre
klempt and
kazoo clear

nude weeds
hearts together jewel
littered grammar
I
to the thrash ceremonies
Waldo compounds looseleaf dollfuzz
homozygous torso
subantarctic
fabrics emit closeknit
bluegreen
subcastes
flipflopped bywords
playschool brickfields
convulsed thropy breathings
Coquitlam
Lougheed
Hatzic
lipteal
microtonal
tempest
downpath
wander somewhere's
beach hallway
folding beachchair
fossilsick nonsense
away in blemish lawn
see light renting garland
see opulently
orangutan tankers
interslice sugarloaf
I'm

anatomical cardamom
asphyxia fogs
itchy wasps
fresh chest bees
heavyset and
decorating lakes
seacoast colour
jiggling buckskin
shallows piper
tyranny's treetop
kilogram of sorry
for what will come
fluids of all tubsized
inattention verdure
I
to the perfumed, quiet bodies
beside sliding water
beside bric-a-brac
tide sag
storm we keen
currant colours
whole beachhead
metathoractic
salmonred grief
tenderfooted
boybody
I'll
give you back
silvery rage
face piles
on agonies

draws me
home birth
kidnapped
hemispheres
acrostic chokepoints
positioning deerskin
in firth
meadow as if
it were a full deer
burning leaves
while whizzing
Rosetta, skin
wonderland
wonderlifts
blink
impossible
I
can only think
in threshold
oolican greasevoice
millilitre
language tailings
pondrests
body obeys
me vanishing
and you in bee costume
disquiet
cervix islet
soaked in
glitter sun
molecules fill

skin watered down
unfashionable gullet
looming storms
unspoken ill even
for what
you say is
sunfish putty on
limestone so
postnominal is
every larynx
haughty lot of
bumblebees are
grandiloquent
bandsaw blades
when I so
much as
vanishing
throats are
sawblade nocturnes
beheading open air
your orb implacable diamond
hanging hair treedwelling
shallotcurl
darkwards
what form
what form
I'm here in
run blood sap
trip patience
gladding
the subject of an act

in our house last
diapers' last tickle
house an organ
the kitchen
autumnal
bee costume
orange graft
outside
neckroom where
smell like snow in
trembling hectares
south by northwest
singling flosculet
paint covered
stars moving
snails dilate
geodynamic eyes
open
to
sun

and I could live my life this way

in strokes of
worktree
glowtops
orange trails
leftover hair
a body's
sonic fictions
is incandescent for

a moment for what
lasting like clamour
one June murknight
pink and blinking
ridiculous crust
caps melting
I could live
drawing curtains
looking out
of sorewater
transcendentals
down to
morning
again to
bind me in
joyride dress
tie me to
lightveins
are
workhouses
heart it's a wonder
I can even
wonder what
what love
lays bare
in me is
energy some
riparian
speakingtube
tasking weight
as snow in

soft sleevecone
does break
upon
thigh
syrup
believes
tongue
at some point
speech
under trees
fall thieving
sleeping cells
and I could live like this
topsoil vials
writing goldmine
continuous
fingernail aroma
burlesquely
open dirt
mooning body
backbites coral
engagement spine
archipelagic when
bronchus shines
when I'm noodling
red mouth toy
bathing buttercups
buttercups tidbit
skinflint pinkish
gamma on nethervert's lid
say

something from hear
believes in utter
parkland
in piecemeal
in purer
in palpitate
engorge
in cloak
between teeth
I do air
still
shoulders
just above
grieving it out
and I could live like this
crescent day
laundry and
bald rye
milk and Cheerios
other planet my
nothing but cool
lavender magnitude
edible slip
from tent to what
boreals' guess
are bodies
because of the birds I told you about
because blooms piss in every direction
because
brainstorm syrup
grouse this age of

triple superconductors
and nonhuman
gorgeousness
a body can be cold
notion blood
blood prosodifies
smalltalk wings
some frustum
wings shaktism because
you theatrically
outside unvisited bush
debar riverbed dada
mattress treeline coconut starfish
and yours is so mine
to reconstruct for us as briefly
as you can say
mineraloids
frogspawns
oral haunts
inglamorous
talk this
joystick earth
subsoils chirping
cerebrovascular
Summer is
so wolves
in meadow portals
sonic
portage, sun
grazer pronoun
rhythm mammal

braids risky
openings
all elegant
tidal thinks
giddy unspeaking must
misspeaks
fungal clots
minor bodies
after
all
these
years
still
nothing
trifled
I
light
rig
bodies
for
pleasure
is
what
you
see
I
give
tongues
what
eaten
is

gone
years
at
my
door
I
stand
in
some
concussed
peerless
air
fed
children
of
mine
bound
symmetry
ruthless
proofs
and
it's
dusk
outside
see
and
raining
see
the
front
of

the
house
thirty
seven
memories
after
so
many
and
nothing
but morselline
dream to be
fucked
and
correspond
ritual fringes
hinterland
parlance
bouncing
off
pubis
fingering
autopilot
lifeforms
spectre
æration in
greenwood
now labiodental
coastal ogres
dressing mosses
gradual

vaultlips
hunting ground
storylines mind
arbour cells
artery vocals suck
demur scriptural nodes
soften footsore balsam
we hold hands anyway
anywhere over anxious
I
to the scrawling acrylic
steepness in starkweather
blackwhite
accept and longing
animus overtexting eyes
you say necks
dwell
sometimes meat
and sometimes touched
and I am yours
and so on
and so
heavier
than whitefish
than comet tail
or I kiss you as suggestions of re
painting and wiping down
some earth
space
some cottage
pine

vernacular acres
parallel lipcut
loads of suet
loads of you
here body
dressing
by laced bricks and
you between house
rows glomerate
tinkering shell
kaleidoscopes
lawn playthings
giddy-go-round
torso too till
exithole too blue
afterbirth
wildfowl
after
cleft love
grasslines
faked tundra by
and by clinging
blue excrete
diphthong pellet
of love and
water
loanwords
lagomorph
landfill hubba
think in clime
in gong think

weigh a feather
child feather-edge
may never know glass
skinlike
deer's sylph arbour
secret legs
scintilla me
hush too
debarkful forest
I am moving
teeth soft
ache in yes
panting
dislikes all
think this ah
this rain
hulking
waterholes
holes where
water goes
trepang ink
I'm embroidering
serpent melon
textile fauna in
wincing pelvises
shuntup stars
fasting vowel
mountains cutthroating
evening
throat sun
melodic cell

death, my
vandalisms
perch torso's
claypool
treelike and
dispersing
wince, please
tentacle embrace
I
octopus costume
thumb architect
windy love me
magnetizer whine
children's urethane
winds traipsed
perky clinging merit
having urchin
fibroblasts
a once
backboneless
rumpus perogy
sweetlooking
whammo boycule
outgassing give
all
I
can
give
exhaustion
eaten riddles
eating surface

persimmon lips
eating sunchair
beyond compression
monomouth galaxials
agave salt
gazing plum notions
my sweet boy
disappearing
midwinter meteorite
chemtrail crumble pie
enormous
buttering
hookworms
checkered and
telegraphing
your
roundhead
soundless
backstitch
pigeonhole
glimpse
bedsides
it's
slaughter
I
told
you
about-shy
slurpwaves
prosodies
bombproof

bedblooded
gobshite
when we
messaround
nebulas
wettest
cosmonautical
imagination is
sparrowing
our animal alones
sail, sail
sail
and I think of next August
that thing I want to show you
when a fire burns outside
and also the word
rocket-propelled
heart
fatigue is
swinge
hectographed
fire
early
I said it
snickering kilowatts
nudethrobbing
memory
swineherd
bends into
tree loss
of murkgrass

the grass
facemask now pancake
shaped birds how
space grows
now as two wills
within me
body
multi-sun
threemoon
futurity
our percussive
story sunrose
your head
just out
between
curio thighs
unword
blood
mellow
uncome
lover's dog
engorged
fainting
bodies
kelp
fit
voice
in
respiratory ways
it was then
then

I tied you to me
tired beachcrumpled child
filthy in sand
weighs mere lips
my lifelong nuisance
is talk endure air
how ritual fingers
moon up against my leg
bushtits or seacucumbers die
unswizzle mouths tune
atonal moment
then venality, cadence
freon violets
kilowatt vanish
as if the whole world
were spores fleeing
the woods' wet animal
grams deep in shade
and somewhere
within beesmudge
cold
cryptograms
simply intimacy
simple food
crisp light visible
corpuscular water stashes
under eyes
gyprock body
papering floral pollen
wood carver orange
blew mores

blew entomologist
breath
I to the headstock
to the intercessions
listen
unsound is
electolyrical
grass is
wet
pictogram hill
lost in dew
I
return with your sock
and disassemble the
mind's agglomerate
mind's wolverine
disassemblage birthmark
your whole body covered red
some fabric cock in wind
leaking armour
had to be our
flavour four
footed revolving
papillaries satdown tinkly
miffed culling
ripped owllight
bronchia think
form a bombsight
think periosteum singing
particle falconry workpiece
two lowcut hills seeking

what stone is
for body
is herd
bracketing
towelcovered
against
body again
glabrous
again colourfully
smother litters
body gooseberry
in which
I say
yes
to
everything
yes
in form
odour
goes
goes back
daylike mild
sun does rock
tendernoon
does
cut timber
pixelglass
tiptoes
your weirdo body
exact in space
leaning on

forehead

a mountain

sorry

boy

sorry

simple

botanical

grief

is lakehurt

waves

prolonging

sorta

lifebook

cream-coloured

seakale sorta

fear stricken

carbonlyrics

ova

and aplomb

and these are things I remember

Coquitlam

glass ravines

Burquitlam

brush like eulogies

Belcarra crags

the tittymags

injectable as blackberries

hinterland stabbings

underpant lichen

refineries

a stump's porn

my furor
my future
voice in secret
pathoformic bodies
outfoxing formatters
wellturned vortices
boomerang gloom
the sweatshirts and
hereword breath a gown
godown bruise
of so many
knuckledraggers
touchingly
short ivy me
pigment
lick me
rulepig
of minuscule
corcule
soul flows
chronophagia
zephyr turn
stingray
archive in
flitter-mouse
crossfire
cross amphibian
auburn flesh
lapilli liquid stills
intravenously my
nothing more

open axe
more galaxy
headlock
littleones
polypore in blankets
in wilderness
plinkferns
plankfires
it's me, boy
it's crawl
overhung yet
formic and afire
consonant
pacific can't
I
to
I
crisping
forms turban
like bodies
anticoagulation
fits shearwater semiholes
wonderfully alloverache
not tactical anymore
circumpolar bonesets
melodies I picture
dik-diks
rushing hibiscus
coldwater sepsis
thumper
birthmark

brachial roam
geode like
my immoveable
heart a boy's
sparrowblasting
a boy's skywriting
festoons his softfooted
torsonic run
moonskinny
inkling
for days
and days
drape light
semée of
Rowan on
Slocan loon
fog horn
luminiferous
handshadows
flock, lapse
long before
astronautics
braze
our
moltenness

&

Mars

Mars was as close as this so long ago
It reminded us of the Neanderthals.
We were stargazing under a beech tree
That could have sheltered United Irishmen.
We were squinting at Mars through binoculars.
'The tree is getting closer to the house.'
'I hope it touches the house before it dies.'
'I hope it touches the house before we die.'

      – Michael Longley

Night & Ox was written during the winter of 2013 and the summer of 2016. During this time, the European Space Agency's Rosetta spacecraft caught up with Comet 67P/Churyumov-Gerasimenko and dropped the Philae lander onto its surface. The lander bounced across the comet's terrain and settled somewhere on its duck-shaped head, where it finally received enough sunlight to emerge from hibernation and contact the Rosetta spacecraft. I first saw the images taken by Rosetta's navigation camera when the comet reached perihelion, its closest approach to the sun. The first images I saw were of a comet deep in shadow surrounded by crisscrossing sunlit jets of gas and dust; a comet's silhouetted underbelly surrounded by faint traces of debris; grainy images of a two-lobed comet uneven in gravity and surrounded by a matrix of stars, particles and a halo of camera noise.

 Within the intervals of these transmissions between Rosetta and Philae, I was learning to be a father. The same sunlight that awoke Philae covered the backyard and kitchen and my two sons at play in our home on Trinity Street, Vancouver, where I wrote most of *Night & Ox*. These images taken by

Rosetta became the mood lighting of a poem that constantly defied containment. When I started the poem, I was just beginning to learn about my boys. I was, as Tom Raworth writes, 'alive and in love' and both completely adrift in this intimacy and completely contained by the rituals of parenting: the bedtime, the snacktime, the naptime, the shit. I wrote *Night & Ox* within these rituals, typing the first lines of the poem with one hand, holding my son Sacha as he slept. With his form attached to mine, the lines took on a shallow and hurried breathing, one of restlessness and the infinitesimal movements of a body bound tightly to a larger form.

Notes and Acknowledgements

For allowing me the time and space to write, I would like to thank the Simon Fraser University Department of English, the Ellen and Warren Tallman Writer in Residence program and the SFU Writer in Residence Committee. I would also like to thank the Canada Council for the Arts and the B.C. Arts Council as well as the incredibly supportive administrative team at Fraser International College, especially Bev Hudson, Christa Ovenell and Sharla Reid.

Thanks to Jonathan Corum for his beautiful *New York Times* article 'Rosetta Follows a Comet through Perihelion' and to the European Space Agency for allowing me to use the images of Comet 67P/Churyumov-Gerasimenko for this book.

I would like to thank the many wonderful people who took the time to read this poem: Stephen Collis, Sarah Dowling, Wiesia Kujawa, Matt Rader (for the Michael Longley poem!), a. rawlings and Jason Starnes.

A couple years ago, Jason Christie and I started sharing poems back and forth on Friday nights, #dadlife. Much of the thinking that went into *Night & Ox* happened within these correspondences and I am forever grateful for his honesty, intelligence and friendship.

I also have to thank my friend Aaron Tucker for reading countless drafts of this poem with such generosity and encouragement.

Donato Mancini was a key editor and brilliant collaborator on this poem, which would simply not have been possible without his guidance and friendship. We spent many nights eating, editing and drinking at Bandidas on Commercial Drive in Vancouver. It was such a pleasure to work in this way. For me, it's the best part of being a poet and I have Donato to thank for this.

Broc Rossell was another important and ingenious collaborator on this poem. I first showed this poem to Broc when I was uncertain about many things in my life and in poetry. He kept me and this poem going through some very intense years. I want to thank him for being such a true friend, editor and collaborator. I could not have written this poem without him.

Thanks to Andrew Zawacki for the back cover blurb and for that long drive from Athens to Spartanburg.

I would like to thank Mark Booth for his beautiful cover art.

This poem developed through a long process of writing through my library and a three-thousand-page word cache from ancestry.com. So many books rotated on and off my desk while writing this book that it's hard to know where to begin. However, there are several books to which this poem owes a great debt. From these books, lines, modes of inquiry and ways of thinking all made their way into this poem: Tim Atkins, Peter Culley, Clark Coolidge, Susan Howe, Fred Moten, Tom Raworth, Lisa Robertson and Cesar Vallejo. The poetry and friendship of Lissa Wolsak was essential to the writing of this poem. Her work is, and will always remain, a guide to my own.

I would like to thank Alana Wilcox for all her work on this book and for her friendship and continued support throughout the years.

I'd also like to thank all the great people at Coach House Books for their energy and kindness.

This is the second book that I've had the pleasure of working with Jeramy Dodds and want to thank him for his editorial vision, attention and kindness. It was such an honour and a joy creating this book with him.

Thank you to Summer Scott, for everything that goes unnoticed. I notice. Love always …

Jordan Scott is the author of *Silt, Blert,* the chapbook *Clearance Process* and, with Stephen Collis, *Decomp.* He was the 2015–16 Writer in Residence at Simon Fraser University. He lives in Port Coquitlam, B.C.

Typeset in Warnock Pro.

Printed at the old Coach House on bpNichol Lane in Toronto, Ontario, on Zephyr Antique Laid paper, which was manufactured, acid-free, in Saint-Jérôme, Quebec, from second-growth forests. This book was printed with vegetable-based ink on a 1965 Heidelberg KORD offset litho press. Its pages were folded on a Baumfolder, gathered by hand, bound on a Sulby Auto-Minabinda and trimmed on a Polar single-knife cutter.

Edited by Jeramy Dodds
Designed by Alana Wilcox
Cover art by Mark Booth, www.markbooth.net
Comet photos by the European Space Agency and the Rosetta
    mission. Images were processed by ESA to bring out details
    of the comet's activity.

Coach House Books
80 bpNichol Lane
Toronto ON M5S 3J4
Canada

416 979 2217
800 367 6360

mail@chbooks.com
www.chbooks.com